HUFF & STITCH

HUFF
STITCH
CLIFF
CARDINAL

PLAYWRIGHTS CANADA PRESS
TORONTO

Huff & Stitch © Copyright 2017 by Cliff Cardinal

For professional or amateur production rights, please contact:
The Gary Goddard Agency
149 Church Street, 2nd Floor
Toronto, ON M5B 1Y4
416.928.0299, www.garygoddardagency.com/apply-for-performance-rights/

LIBRARY AND ARCHIVES CANADA CATALOGUING IN PUBLICATION
Cardinal, Cliff, 1985-, author
    Huff & stitch / by Cliff Cardinal.

A play.
Issued in print and electronic formats.
ISBN 978-1-77091-746-0 (softcover).--ISBN 978-1-77091-747-7 (PDF).--
ISBN 978-1-77091-748-4 (EPUB).--ISBN 978-1-77091-749-1 (Kindle)

    I. Title. II. Title: Huff and stitch.

PS8605.L5574H84 2017   C812'.6   C2016-907872-8
                                         C2016-907873-6

We acknowledge the financial support of the Canada Council for the Arts, the Ontario Arts Council (OAC), the Ontario Media Development Corporation, and the Government of Canada through the Canada Book Fund for our publishing activities.

Canada Council Conseil des arts
for the Arts   du Canada

ONTARIO ARTS COUNCIL
CONSEIL DES ARTS DE L'ONTARIO
an Ontario government agency
un organisme du gouvernement de l'Ontario

Ontario
Ontario Media Development
Corporation

Dedicated to Tantoo and Riel and Nicole.

AUTHOR'S NOTE

I never thought I'd see the day that my work was published. I never thought it would be produced. I had planned to burn my plays. You know, to punish a sick world by depriving it of my beautiful work. (My agent assures me the money is the same.)

I started writing *Stitch* when I was twenty-two. I was living in a roach-infested basement. There was no natural light—I wrote under fluorescence. I shared the apartment with a prostitute who paid me ten dollars a trick to rent the bedroom. I'd be writing late at night or early in the morning, get a knock at the door, and have to walk around outside for fifteen minutes and write in a notebook. Imagine following a mascaraed stranger into a dank basement and seeing cheerful little me making myself scarce, skittering out like one of the roaches: "Have a nice time."

Then I'd come back and write until I had to go to work for a special event company. I carried furniture by day, barely ate, just smoked.

The central image in *Stitch* came from a dream my mom had. The form was influenced by VideoCabaret, Linda Griffiths's *Baby Finger*, and Daniel Brooks and Daniel MacIvor's *Monster*. I was reading a lot of Hubert Selby Jr., Chuck Palahniuk, and Irvine Welsh. Leanna Brodie introduced me to a few dramaturges. I started working with her husband, Jovanni Sy. He's a very generous collaborator and he's become a good friend.

I was just beginning to write me. What scared me and what turned me on. I was writing what embarrassed me. I tried the first person and I heard my voice.

Then there was *huff*.

I've been touring this show for a few years now. Along the way I did this interview with a French journalist who asked if in writing *huff* I had any "denunciations." Not a word you hear every day, but the ESL-style question is a pretty succinct one. The answer is yes. I don't have anything to say. I don't know how the world is supposed to work. I don't have any ideas. Give me the floor for an hour and I'll shit in a beer bottle. I had denunciations. We have disparaging rates of youth suicide. Sexual abuse is a dark part of our national history. First Nation's people are still fighting to reclaim parts of our culture that were stolen in genocide. *huff* is a punk show. It's a fuck you to a society that would put our little brothers and sisters' backs against the wall. I wanted to throw a brick.

I was singing in a punk band. I was inspired by *Jackass* the TV show—hurt myself to make my friends laugh. I was obsessed with telling stories about outsiders, people who do weird stuff to make a connection. I thought our most taboo subculture was First Nations' kids abusing solvents, at high risk of suicide. I wrote a short story.

I carried the story for four years and made a few attempts at writing a play. I didn't have much success until Patti Shaughnessy booked it for the Ode'min Giizis festival in Peterborough.

That gave me a year to write and create a new solo play. I got some money through the Theatre Creators' Reserve. Native Earth programmed it in the Weesageechak festival. Jovanni was going to dramaturge again but I wasn't ever ready to show him anything. Opening night was approaching and we didn't have time to get into our old rhythms of notes and drafts. Most of the dramaturgy happened in rehearsals at the Centre for Indigenous Theatre by Karin Randoja. That being said, I owe a debt to the creativity of Mason Wales, David Geary, Elizabeth Kantor, and especially Karin, whose directorial vision was the basis for the two proceeding productions and tours.

When I perform the show I think about the kids in the story: little shit disturbers with fierce imaginations. I want to do a play that they would love. That's why there's so much cussing. That's why I splash the audience with tomatoes. That's why I don't care what people think about it.

HUFF

Huff was first produced by Cardinal/Kantor Productions on June 21 and 22 at the Gordon Best Theatre, Peterborough, as part of the Ode'min Giizis Festival. It featured the following cast and creative team:

Director: Karin Randoja
Designer and Stage Manager: Elizabeth Kantor
Performer: Cliff Cardinal
Technician: Em Glasspool

The play was remounted by Native Earth Performing Arts in 2015 and later toured throughout Canada in 2016.

CHARACTERS

Wind

WIND enters. He has a plastic bag over his head. It's duct-taped around his throat to create an airtight seal.

WIND: Turn off your fucking cellphone.
Put the remote down.
This is an interruption of your regularly scheduled program.
Don't worry though.
Your normal show will be on again soon.
This isn't life and death.
Not for you.

Where I am is in my apartment not trying to take a plastic bag off my head.
It's duct-taped to my throat.
And my hands are handcuffed behind my back.
The key to my handcuffs is stashed in the top cupboard where I can't get at it.
Anoxia is the word for when your brain is deprived of oxygen.
Anoxia will kill you somewhere between four and six minutes.
You'll pass out after three.
I've been in this bag for two.
Actually about one minute and fifty-seven seconds.

WIND breathes. The plastic bag crumples around his face.

Now.
Definitely.
It's been five minutes.
My breath feels warm inside the mask.
Like a baby's . . .

This is a suicide attempt.
I say "attempt" but it's looking pretty good.
I should know.
I've done this before.

> WIND *hears a gentle whisper through the plastic bag: "Breathe."*
> *He looks around but can't find where the voice is coming from.*

When you hear something like that it doesn't mean anything.
You probably made it up.
Maybe a hallucination brought on by your brain screaming out for oxygen.
I'm ninety per cent sure that's what you are.
"Hi, imaginary friends!"

> *He hears the whisper again: "Breathe."*

Next time you hear it the voice is familiar.
Like a TV show that's gone off the air.

> *A third time: "Breathe." He shrugs at the plastic bag with his shoulders but can't remove his death mask. He falls to the floor trying to get the bag off.*

I think about yelling at myself.
About cursing my own stupidity.
But I don't want to give myself the satisfaction.
Anyway, that's how I got here.
Really, there's a perfectly rational explanation for all of this.

(to an audience member) Hey, can you get this off me?
Seriously.
This isn't a metaphor.
If you don't help me I'll suffocate right here.

> WIND *enters the audience. He bows to an audience member who removes the mask and duct tape and handcuffs. (If the audience*

member says anything aside from "yes," WIND goes to someone else.) WIND takes the handcuffs back.

I'll take those.

WIND thrusts the plastic bag back into the audience member's hands.

And this.
Hold onto this for me.
And don't give it back no matter what I say.
Okay?
I need you.
Thanks.

He goes back to the stage. He gives thanks.

Hiye hiye.

He turns back to the audience.

Trickster.
See, for my people, "Trickster" is a real thing.
Ask anyone's kohkum.
If you listen, you can hear the lessons.
And through the generations we've heard the lessons so many times, we came up with a word for it: Trickster.
That one drink too many before the drive home: Trickster.
That questionable piece of ass you tapped *au naturel*: Trickster.
That the very story that brought you into the darkness is the only one that can lead you back to the light: Trickster.
When you've got a plastic bag on your head, what you're doing is rebreathing the same breath until it chokes you.
The breath I'm breathing is a story that began a long time ago . . . in the eighties.

One day a young warrior on the hunt met a beautiful girl.
He'd known her since she was a child but looked on her with new eyes.

At a time when all the young warriors were meeting their future wives, Tracey was the most beautiful girl Michael had ever seen.
She had the kind of beauty that tribes went to war for.
A beauty that pulled the air from an Indian's lungs.
With great respect and trepidation Michael approached and requested permission to begin courting:

MIKE: Tracey, why are you so stuck up?

TRACEY: Why you gotta be like that?
Is it so hard to just be happy?

WIND: *(to audience)* The girl had many suitors but accepted the young warrior's request because . . .
But accepted the young warrior's request because . . . because Trickster.
Before long the warrior had acquired enough firewood for the winter and a lodge big enough for them both.
When he was ready he brought her there and asked her to marry him.
With joy in her heart the beautiful girl went to her mother to tell of the young warrior's proposal.

TRACEY: Mama, I'm pregnant.

KOHKUM: Ah shit.
Here we go.
It's because you don't listen.
Now here you are in a way . . . knocked up . . . up the stick.
And I'll tell you something about that man of yours for free: Way he treats you?
He's either dumb, stupid, or just ain't got no good sense.

TRACEY: But, Mama, I love him.

KOHKUM: Ah shit.
It's because you don't listen.

WIND: *(to audience)* So the young warrior and the beautiful girl were wed; and they were happy . . .

No one knows how the young warrior drew Trickster's attention.

Maybe one of those little curses you think you walk away from.

Ever said "I love you" and weren't sure you meant it?

Ever stolen something and gotten away with it?

Ever walked the streets at night and had nowhere to go?

Trickster is waiting for you there.

I don't have the antidote.

I don't know how it stops and I don't know how things change.

But there is one thing we know attracts Trickster: fear.

And for all the strong, powerful ways the young warrior was, he was also afraid.

Soon Trickster preyed on him in his dreams.

The young warrior turned cruel.

He beat the girl, took away her hope.

He became less a warrior and more a demon.

The girl was trapped and turned to the bottle.

When her first son Charles was born the midwife could smell the alcohol on the baby.

The girl's mother, the baby's kohkum, came to the young couple with medicine and in ceremony showed the two the way out of the darkness.

KOHKUM sings.

The girl quit drinking and the young warrior promised never to be so cruel again.

Six years passed and they had another son.

And then another.

But Trickster is patient.

Soon the young warrior chased every hot girl on the rez totally unchecked.

Soon the girl turned back to the bottle.

Soon the young couple was back in the darkness where they began.

When the young warrior abandoned the beautiful girl and her three children to the winter Trickster was ready.

MIKE: Sons, I love you.
Always remember that.
I got some bad news.
Your mom is dead.
That means she's gone and she's never coming back.

WIND: But, Dad, she's coming back.
She just went to the store or out some place.

MIKE: She took herself away from us.
Went into the woods with a rope.
Tied it around her neck.
Stopped breathing.
We're here.
Together.
Warriors, sons.
When I was a kid nobody ever stood up and cheered for me.
But that's not the way it's gonna be for you.
There's gonna be some changes.
Real changes.
I'm not gonna be drinkin so much anymore.
After this.

He drinks.

Your kohkum's gonna be helpin out more.
And your auntie Donna's gonna be movin in.

KOHKUM: No, Mike.
Auntie Donna's no auntie.
Can't you let my daughter rest before you go moving your other woman in?

MIKE: Kohkum, you're very confused.

KOHKUM: You drove my daughter to kill herself.
You did.
This is your fault.

MIKE: Old woman, if you hadn't lost your daughter today I'd—

WIND: *(to audience)* And somewhere in all of this me and my brothers were to find our way.

> *At the radio station.*

TRICKSTER: Thank you for listening to Shit Creek Radio, your voice for when you're up Shit Creek and you don't have a paddle.
The weather has been cold and weird recently.
Cold as in fifty below.
Weird as in there have been reports of strange whisperings in the wind.
Voices echo faintly in the darkness.
It's some real *X-Files* stuff goin on in Shit Creek.
Of course most have been quick to dismiss the reports as the ravings of madmen and elders in early onset dementia; but don't discredit the reports.
For wise men listen to fools, not the other way around.
Is that Pink Floyd or the Bible?

WIND: *(to HUFF)* Get the bag ready.
Last time the hose started flowing and you got gas all over yourself.

HUFF: Is she coming?

WIND: Not yet.
I'll give you the signal.

HUFF: What's the signal?

WIND: Don't worry.
You'll know it.

> *WIND smacks HUFF upside the head.*

HUFF: Ow!

WIND: Come on, let's go, that was the signal.

HUFF: Hey, wait up!

WIND: Hurry up, don't look back!

HUFF: You didn't have to hit me.

WIND: Yes I did.
Teacher would have fucked you up if she caught you siphoning gas from her car.
Man this thing is heavy.
You're really good at siphoning gas.
Siphoning gas must be your sacred gift from Creator.

HUFF: No, siphoning gas isn't my sacred gift from Creator.

WIND: Yeah, what's your sacred gift from Creator?

HUFF: You know that feeling you get when you laugh?
You know how inside it feels real good and everything?
I can give that to someone.
Just by blowing.
Like this.

    HUFF blows; WIND feels laughter but doesn't laugh.

WIND: Whoa, how'd you do that?

HUFF: What's your sacred gift from Creator?

WIND: I don't think I have one.

HUFF: Yeah.
Everyone has a sacred gift from Creator.
We just have to find yours.

WIND: Maybe it's . . . shoplifting.
Yeah, shoplifting is my sacred gift from Creator.

HUFF: Awesome!

WIND: *(to audience)* Hey!
Whoa!
Imaginary friends!
This is our favourite place.
Only we know about it so we get to make the rules.
The abandoned motel by the highway.
You gotta crawl in through a hole in the roof and you gotta swear on a stack of Bibles you won't tell anyone what happens here.
Swear . . . no, like, swear.
Think of your favourite swear word and on the count of three we're all gonna swear em.
Ready?
One . . . two . . . I'm serious, you guys . . . three: COCKSUCKING MOTHERFUCKER!
Now that everyone's sworn in I can show you the rest.

This is the cockpit where we effortlessly glide our vessel through time and space.
This is the kitchen; but it's magical too.
Say, you want some . . . delicious lasagna?
All you have to do is put animal foreskins in the top, press the buttons on the control panel, and bam!
Out it comes.
Unfortunately we don't have any animal foreskins right now.
Oh, and check it out: it's Charles's porn collection.

HUFF: What we should do, is we should hide some of it, and watch him freak out.

WIND: Yeah!
Great idea!

WIND hides CHARLES's porn in the magic oven.

Shhhh!

WIND picks up the bag of gas.

(to audience) You wanna go first?

Beat.

Okay.
Gas tastes like metal but also like being scared.
Like someone's screaming in your face.

WIND screams in silence.

He takes a big breath from the bag.

Another.

The first thing that happens is you feel like you're watching everything on TV.
Only you've already seen the show.
So you feel nice and safe cuz you know everything that's gonna happen.

He takes another big breath from the bag.

Then you hallucinate.
Big.
I can hear my name in the wind.
"Wiiiiiiiiiiiiiind."

WIND laughs. He laughs again—dry heaves a little . . .

Sometimes you puke on yourself.
It's awesome.

Sniff.

It's the funnest thing you'll ever do.
If you're not too much of a pussy.
Then after a while you're not watching the show anymore.
You're part of it.

WIND nods off.

He wakes up in Hockey Night in Canada*!*

HOCKEY ANNOUNCER HARRY: Good evening, ladies and gentlemen, and welcome to game seven of the Stanley Cup Finals.
Leafs are down one in the third period with both Toronto Maple Leaf goals coming from the rookie from Shit Creek, Ontario.

HOCKEY ANNOUNCER DICK: We're surprised to see him in tonight's game after disclosing the upper body injury he sustained in a fight with his dad over the recycling earlier in the season, but here he is single-handedly keeping the Toronto Maple Leafs in the game.
What a performance, Harry!
And he's only an Indian!

HOCKEY ANNOUNCER HARRY: Good point, Dick.
Here he is coming down the right side.
He curls back looking for his brother.
Can't find him—
He cuts towards the net.
He steps out in front . . .
He shoots . . . he scores!
Leafs tie!
Leafs tie!

Buzz!

HOCKEY ANNOUNCER DICK: That buzzer signals the end of regulation time—this game is going to sudden death overtime!

HOCKEY ANNOUNCER DICK holds out the bag of gas as a microphone. WIND takes a breath of the noxious fumes before answering any questions.

HOCKEY ANNOUNCER HARRY: Here's the rookie now!
What were you thinking with the game at the end of your stick?

Huff.

WIND: Nothing.

HOCKEY ANNOUNCER HARRY: Nothing?

WIND: Yeah, that's the point.
I wasn't thinkin bout nothing!

HOCKEY ANNOUNCER HARRY: Seems short-sighted.
Good luck on the English test tomorrow!
And . . . wake up!
Seriously, kid.
You better wake up!

HUFF: Wake up . . . Charles is coming.

WIND: Oh fuck, Charles!

CHARLES enters, smiling.

CHARLES: Hear what happened to the hamster in sixth grade class?
Martin.
The hamster.
He's dead.
Somebody kill im.
Found bloody scissors next to the cage.
Somebody cut his head off.

CHARLES can't find his porn.

Where is it?
What'd you do with it?

WIND: Your porno?
We don't know where it is.
But we'll give it back.
First we're going to have to administer a little test.
The FAS test.

CHARLES: Huh?

WIND: FAS.
Means you got holes in your brain cuz Mom drank while she was pregnant with you.

> HUFF *laughs.*

HUFF: She must not have loved you very much, huh.

WIND: So how bout it?

CHARLES: Give me my porno back!
I don't want to play your stupid game.

WIND: I see.
Interesting.
I'm going to make a note of that.

> WIND *pantomimes writing in a fake notebook. He mouths the word he's pretending to write: moron.*

Don't worry about it.
It's technical . . .
Do you know what technical means?

> CHARLES *chokes* WIND.

It's okay.
It's not part of the test.

HUFF: Let him go.
He can't breathe.

> *HUFF wrestles* CHARLES's *hand off* WIND's *throat.* CHARLES *searches for his porn.*

CHARLES: You better not have done anything with it.

WIND: Okay.
We'll give it back.
. . . After the FAS test.
First question: spell "cat."
Come on.
"Cat."
It's three letters.
I'll give you the first one.
"C."
You got two more.
You can do it.
Come on . . . unlimited guesses.
If you can't pass we have to come back and give you the Down syndrome test.

CHARLES: I got a test.
Let's see how much fun we can have with this beer bottle.

WIND: Okay, fine, Charles.
It's in the magic oven.

> CHARLES *finds his porno. He groans with relief.*

CHARLES: Good.
Wanna see?

CHARLES *hands a magazine to* WIND.

Take your dick out.
Only faggots don't jerk off.
Take your dick out.

CHARLES *sees* HUFF.

You too, take your little dick out.

HUFF *looks at the audience. He unzips his fly—*

WIND: Hey, wait, Charles . . . I got a game.
I got a new game.
It's called "smoking."

WIND *takes out a cigarette, flicks a lighter.*

CHARLES: Gimme.

WIND: You want it?
Here!

WIND *jabs at* CHARLES *with the lit cigarette.* CHARLES *chases* WIND.

Okay, here.

WIND *throws the cigarette on the ground.*

(to audience) I toss the lit cigarette on a dog-eared porno magazine soiled
in semen and gasoline.
The smut publication ignites in a flash.

WIND *holds the burning magazine at arm's length.*

(to CHARLES) Quick, Charles!
Come on it!

(to audience) I throw the burning porno magazine out the window.
It lands in the snow and is just about to burn out when the wind screams through the trees.
The pages turn to wings as the burning magazine becomes a raven.
The raven flies back onto the windowsill and lands before returning to flame and igniting the curtains.
Trickster.

    WIND *escapes from the motel.*

Outside, Charles is gone.
Me and my little brother watch the motel burn.
The black smoke obscures the trees and the night sky and breaks in the wind and you can see the stars through the swirling darkness.

(to HUFF*)* Awesome.
We should do this again sometime.

HUFF: But . . . we can't.
It's gone.

WIND: Oh yeah.
. . . The school then.

HUFF: Awesome!

WIND: Come on, let's go home.

    Sees something . . .

Hey.

Do you see that?
It looks like a cat or a skunk.
Skunk?
Skuuunk!

The SKUNK *stands poised. He licks the air! He holds his tail like a shotgun!* .

SKUNK: Whoa!
Whoa!
Whoa!
Don't move, man.
Don't you fuckin move.
You think I won't do this shit?
I will, man.
I'll give you a mouthful of my sweet skunk juices right fuckin here.

HUFF: Whoa!
Skunks can talk?

SKUNK: That's right, skunks can talk.
And I'm talkin to you, motherfucker!

WIND: Please!
Let us go!
We're only children.

SKUNK: Really?
You look like brothers.

WIND: We are.

SKUNK: But you just said you were "only" children.
I've already caught you in a lie.
This is not going well for you.

HUFF: Please, we don't mean to hurt anyone.

SKUNK: Really?
What do you call that?
I call it a goddamn forest fire!
Now here's what you don't know: somebody dies in this fire.

Yeah, that's right.
I've foreseen the shit.

The SKUNK opens his eyes wide to emphasize the clarity of his vision.

This fireman named . . . Stevie Windsor . . . is gonna come out here to put out this fire, and, in the process, suffer a heart attack and die.
You know what that means?

WIND: He was probably a diabetic?

SKUNK: It means restitutions have to be made, motherfucker!

HUFF: It's not our fault!
The flaming porno magazine turned into a raven—

SKUNK: I'm going to have to cut you off right there.
You're telling me that some gay porno you guys were rockin turned into Raven?

WIND: It wasn't gay porno.

SKUNK: But you just said it was "flaming."
Really?
Is that really what you're worried about?
Someone's gonna think you're a homosexual?
You got bigger problems here, kid!

HUFF: Please, can we go home?
We just want to go home.

SKUNK: All right.
You seem like nice enough kids so I'm going to let your lucky asses off the hook with a warning.
But heed my words, motherfuckers!

The SKUNK lets down his tail.

WIND: *(to audience)* That's when our dog Angelina shows up in protection mode.
(to ANGELINA) Angelina, no!

ANGELINA, *the boys' dog, sees the hostage situation.*

ANGELINA: Leave my brothers alone!

SKUNK: You lied, motherfuckers!

The SKUNK *sprays everyone! The* SKUNK *flees!*

WIND: *(to audience)* The skunk is gone, but Smell remains.

SMELL: You know what the worst part about smelling bad is?
You never feel like you deserve to be anywhere.
And you don't, you piece of shit.
You can't just walk into class smelling like rancid fish or rotten eggs or the inside of a skunk's asshole?
Who do you think you are?

ANGELINA: Oh the smell!
It's huge!
I'm useless.
If I weren't so stupid, stupid, stupid.
I'm no good.
A no-good girl.
No!
Good!
Girl!

WIND: You stupid bitch, Angelina!
What were you thinking?

WIND kicks ANGELINA.

HUFF: It's not her fault.
She didn't mean for us to get sprayed.

HUFF smells himself.

Now what do we do?

WIND: Kohkum.
Let's go see Kohkum.

SMELL: *(to audience)* Kohkum is the owner of the local store.
That makes her the hub of commerce and knower of lore.
Arcane and domestic.

KOHKUM: *(from over the counter)* Ah shit.
Close that damn door behind you.
You're gonna give your grandmother hyper thermal.

SMELL: Hey, Kohkum.
I bet when you take your false teeth out you give a great blow job.
Would I win that bet?

KOHKUM: Pew!
Stink!
Nosums, the smell.
. . . You got sprayed by Skunk.
Nosums, skunks are powerful messengers.
They show your shame.
Here, take this sacred medicine tobacco.
It will protect you until the smell dissipates.

KOHKUM gives WIND a cigarette. She's taken aback by the smell.

And here: a jar of tomatoes.
Go on now.
Take a bath.
Go.

KOHKUM looks to the audience.

(to audience) Not you!
You just wait right there.
That's right.
I see you.
You're here to take me to spirit world.
No.
You're here to help my nosums!
Good thing.
Cuz I'm no good.
Listen to this.

KOHKUM walks around the counter.

Don't rush me.

When she's ready.

First time my daughter got beat up by Mike I picked her up.
Took her home.
Took care of her.
Then I sent my son round to talk to Mike.
Found him at the bar.
Gave him a lickin.
Second time: same thing.
I pick her up.
Take her home.
Then I go down to my son's place and, shit, here he's passed out drunk.
I'm thinkin: Who can I call?
You know: to beat my daughter's husband.

Ah shit, Kohkum!
That who you are?
Going around trying to fix everybody?
Or do I be like Duck?

How the water falls off their back, there.
You tell me.

> *Beat.*

Ah shit.
If she's gonna go back to him that's what she's gonna do.
If my son's gonna drink that's what he's gonna do.
If the boys are gonna steal Lysol—
Ah, shit.
I don't want to talk about that.

> WIND *lights the cigarette.*

HUFF: You're gonna smoke up the sacred tobacco?
But Kohkum said to keep that safe until the smell "dissipates."

WIND: That mean you don't want any?

> WIND *hands the cigarette to* HUFF. HUFF *smokes of the sacred tobacco. He coughs.*

HUFF: Awesome.

> *At home,* WIND *creaks the kitchen door open. The television blares. He speaks to the audience, almost in a whisper:*

WIND: My dad is my favourite person in the world.
He can do anything.
He went to prison when I was a little kid.
So I don't mean to start anything: but my dad could prob'ly kick your dad's ass.
But all that kicking guys' dad's asses makes him pretty tired.
You can come over but it's better not to bother him while he's watching TV.

WIND sneaks around his father and grabs a bowl, then runs down into the basement.

(to SMELL) Hey, Smell, come down to the basement.
I wanna show you something.

SMELL: Hey, guys, what's up?

WIND pours the tomatoes into a bowl.

What's up with the tomatoes?
Playing awfully close to the tomatoes, don't you think?
I don't like this.
I don't like this.
Help!
Somebody!
Help me!
Help!
I'm melting!

WIND squishes his hands into the tomatoes and bathes up to his elbows.

HUFF: Basement's cold.

WIND: We'll be fast.

HUFF: Tomatoes are cold.

WIND: Squish yourself around in them.
Like this.
It's fun.
Look: I'm Mom.

WIND lies perfectly still, imitating a corpse. His eyes open, he plays dead for a long time. Too long.

HUFF: Stop it!
Cut it out!
I hate it when you—

> *HUFF hits WIND, splashing tomatoes into the audience. WIND is dripping in tomato juice.*

WIND: *(to audience)* Oh my God, did I get you?
If any of this gets on any of you . . . um . . . you're part of the movement now.
Yeah!
Consider this your Indian test of bravery . . . and you passed!
High-five!

> *WIND high-fives someone in the audience, splattering them with tomato juice.*

Now you know what it's like to be an Indian!
How about a round of applause for our new brothers and sisters?

> *WIND applauds. A thin mist of tomato juice sprays the audience; the pungent smell lingers for the rest of the story.*

And if you're still upset . . .
Wait'll you see what happens next.

> *MIKE enters.*

MIKE: What the . . .
You . . .
Hahaha!
You got sprayed by—
Then you—
Hahaha!
Donna!
Woman!
Woman!

Woman!
Look!
My boys!
They got sprayed by Skunk and now look: they're already takin a bath
in tomatoes.

    DONNA squawks!

DONNA: Oh my gawd!
Ever cute these boys a yers!
Ever real industrious.
I'm gonna cook you two a special dinner.

    DONNA picks up the phone.

Hey, Cherise.
Pepperoni.
Bacon.
Mushrooms.
Extra cheese and one—
No.
Two litres of Coke.
Thanks, Cherise.

    DONNA hangs up the phone.

Mike, ever cute those boys a yers.
Ever real industrious those boys a yers.

MIKE: Woman, you just said that twenty minutes ago.
Will you get over it?

DONNA: Hey, skunk-tamers.
You wanna play Sega Genesis with your dad?

MIKE: Woman . . .

DONNA: Come on!
The boys wanna play Sega with their daddy.

WIND: Yeah, Dad!
Sega!

MIKE: Okay, get me a beer.

WIND: You're the best, Dad!

    WIND gives a beer to his dad. (Not before sneaking a sip.)

(to audience) Do you have Sega Genesis?
It's our thirty-two-bit status symbol.
Our oasis by the beach.
Our adopted mother.

(to the game console) Hey, Big Mama Sega Genesis!
You ready to go?

BIG MAMA SEGA GENESIS: How you doin, baby?
You wanna play *Sonic the Hedgehog*?

MIKE: Hockey.

BIG MAMA SEGA GENESIS: I was talkin to the child.
Child, you wanna play hockey?
Anything for you, baby.

    WIND scores.

DONNA: Nice one!
Gettim!

WIND: Yes!
Nice one, eh, Dad?
Pretty sweet goal.

MIKE: Don't rub it in.

DONNA: No, rub it in!
Teach him a lesson!

WIND scores again.

MIKE: Cheap goal.
Game cheats.

BIG MAMA SEGA GENESIS: Cheat?
If cheatin means makin it easier for my babies while hindering their opposition then I'm guilty.

WIND scores again.

DONNA: Mike, don't.

WIND: *(to audience)* My father moves like a wolf.
He grabs Big Mama Sega Genesis and throws her across the room.
And Big Mama Sega Genesis says:

BIG MAMA SEGA GENESIS screams as she flies at the wall:

BIG MAMA SEGA GENESIS: SEGA!

WIND: . . . and lands: splash!
Right in Angelina's dish when she's drinking.

ANGELINA: Sex and violence!
Sex and violence!

MIKE: I'm going out.
Get the kids to bed.

DONNA: Mike, it's just a game.
We're having a nice time.

MIKE: Thought you wanted to be a mother.
Now's your fuckin chance.

> *MIKE leaves; DONNA follows him to the door.*

DONNA: Mike—
That's not—
You can't just—
I wanna go too!
Mike!
. . . Time for bed, kids.

HUFF: That's my mom's sweater.

DONNA: Your dad was gonna throw it out so I kept it.

WIND: My mom's a lot prettier than you.

DONNA: Time for bed, kids.

> *WIND climbs onto the chair.*

WIND: *(to audience)* Little kids are cruel.
We know when you're beat.
Me and my little brother can torment you like a horde of blackflies.

(to DONNA) Donna, can we watch a movie?
Donna, can we have ice cream?
Donna, can we go to McDonald's?
Donna, Charles is trying to light a cat on fire.

DONNA: Jesus Christ, Charles.
Let that cat alone.

WIND: *(to audience)* She's waiting at the door.
Watching for my father to come home.
All she wants in the world is for me and my brother to go to sleep.

HUFF: Donna!
Donna!
Donna!
Donna!
Donna!
Donna!
Donna!

DONNA: Stop it!
Awus!
I'll make you a deal.
If you're good, and you go to bed, I'll give you candy for breakfast.
That's right, candy in your Frosted Flakes.
Just please go to sleep.

> *DONNA closes the bedroom door and goes into the bathroom. She runs the shower and takes her clothes off. She lathers. She sings.*

> *She hears someone come in.*

Jus'quaw!
I'm in the shower.

> *They don't leave.*

I'm in the shower, I said!

> *She peaks out from behind the shower curtain.*

Charles, get out!
Stop looking at me.
Stop it!
Get out, I said!
You fucking little pervert, Charles!

> *She looks down at his penis.*

Put that dick away.
Stop it.
Stop doing that.
Charles.
Stop looking at me.
Fucking stop it!
Get out!
Get out!
Get out!

> CHARLES *doesn't leave.* DONNA *ducks behind the shower curtain when he comes.*

Clean that up!

> *He leaves.*

Get back here and clean that up!
No, no.
Go.
Get out.
Get out.
You fucking little pervert, Charles.

> DONNA *gets out, wraps herself in a towel. The door opens again.*

You're supposed to be in bed.
Get in bed or no candy for breakfast.

HUFF: There's a monster in my room.

> DONNA *looks under the bathroom sink and hands* HUFF *a bottle of Lysol.*

Here!
Now go to sleep.

WIND: A full bottle of Lysol?
You're the best, Donna!

TRICKSTER takes the microphone.

TRICKSTER: Thank you for listening to Shit Creek Radio, your voice for when you're up Shit Creek and you don't have a paddle.
Shit Creek News has learned a fireman died responding to the blaze at the White Pines Motel.
It was confirmed Stevie Windsor was also a diabetic.
This could have contributed to this tragic incident.
Officials have declared the fire arson.
A criminal investigation is officially underway.
Whoever did this will officially be getting their ass kicked pretty hard.
Trickster.
In the weather, it's going to be another cold and windy day.

WIND wakes up.

WIND: *(to audience)* You may be able to tell by the gas huffing and the arson but me and my brother are products of the reserve school system.
Yay!
Yay!
Yay!
Every morning the children pour into the school brimming with optimism and a love of learning.

WIND animates the children with beer bottles as puppets.

HUFF: Know what?
I love teacher.
She's so nice.

WIND: Really?
I think she's a dyke bitch.

HUFF: No way!

TRISHA: Know what?
I saw your sister at my house last night.
She had sex with all three of my brothers.

DEBBIE: No way!

PIERRE: Know what?
The statistical rate of suicide for First Nations living on the reserve is highest in the world.
Yes way!

WIND: *(to audience)* Hey, look over there at Tommy.
He thinks he's so much better because he's white.
Fuckin white kid.
I fuckin hate white kids.
Look at him with his white shoes and his white Trapper Keeper and his white lunch.
I heard he has Sega *and* Super Nintendo.

TRISHA: Hey, Tommy!

WIND plays TOMMY like he has Down syndrome.

TOMMY: Henh . . .

WIND: *(to audience)* Fuckin white kid.
I fuckin hate white kids.
Now I'm no racist . . .

WIND smiles. He hears the teacher coming . . .

You have to be a special kind of person to teach in the reserve school system.
You have to basically be a saint.
Or have some weird control issues and a terrible resumé.
On the first day she said to call her "Ms. R."

But we gave her a spirit name.
May I present, from Milton, Ontario: Miss Ratface.

MISS RATFACE: Good morning, boys and girls.
I have a very exciting lesson planned for you all today.

HUFF *hugs* MISS RATFACE.

Oh hugs.
Yes, hugs are nice.
It's appropriate to hug someone you care about.
There.
Okay, that's enough hugging.
That's enough—
Stop hugging me.

WIND: Miss Ratface, how come you don't have any kids?

MISS RATFACE: If everyone could just divert your attention to the board.

WIND: I mean: Can you not have kids?

MISS RATFACE: That's not a very appropriate question to be asking a woman of a certain age—

WIND: Are you one of those Lebanese?

MISS RATFACE: I believe the word you are looking for is "lesbian."

WIND: I knew it!
You're a lesbian.
Miss Ratface is a lesbian!

HUFF: Miss Ratface is a lesbian.

WIND: Lesbian!

HUFF: Lesbian!

TRISHA: Lesbian

PIERRE: L'esbian!

TOMMY: Henh . . .

MISS RATFACE: You!
Did you read from the book last night?
No.
Of course not.
We knew you wouldn't have.
Didn't we, everybody?
Didn't we, Tommy?
Didn't we know this boy wouldn't have his homework done?

TOMMY: Henh . . .

MISS RATFACE: Let me ask you something: Are you stupid?
I don't think so but it's hard to tell.
If you haven't done the homework then how could you possibly have
anything to add to the conversation?
Anything you say is irrelevant.
Do you know what that word means?
That's right, bud.
It means you don't matter.
Would you like to put that word on the board for us so we can all remember it?
No, of course not.
You can't spell it.
Because somebody's parents didn't stress education . . .

HUFF: Leave my brother alone, you dyke bitch.

MISS RATFACE: Excuse me?
Would you like to repeat that?

HUFF: I said, leave my brother alone, dyke bitch crusty cunt scab-sucker.

MISS RATFACE: You!
Up to the front of the class.

This little boy isn't getting enough attention at home.
So we're all going to help him with that.
Who knows "The Care Bear Stare?"
Ready, Care Bears?
Stare!

> *The class stares at* HUFF.

> HUFF *poops his pants.*

Oh my goodness.
Did you . . . defecate?

HUFF: No.
. . . I pooped my pants.

MISS RATFACE: Take your little brother to the office.
Now!

> WIND *takes* HUFF *into the hall.*

HUFF: I don't want to go back to class.

WIND: Why, cuz you shit yourself?
How come you always gotta shit your pants?
Why can't you be normal and break stuff?
Or cut your arms?
Why you always gotta shit yourself?

(to audience) We walk home in the cold and the smell follows us the entire way there.

SMELL: Hey, guys.

You know, when you drowned me in a vat of tomatoes, I kinda thought that you didn't want to be my friend.

I didn't think you'd invite me over again so soon.

It's almost like you want me to tell everyone all about you.

WIND: Fuck off, Smell.

(to audience) In the basement my little brother knows the drill.

He scrapes shit out of his tighty-whities using cold toilet water.

    HUFF *cleans his underwear.*

HUFF: I like skipping school.

Remember the time Mom let us skip school and took us to the beach?

WIND: No.

Don't remember.

HUFF: Really?

It was just last year?

WIND: Nope.

Don't remember.

HUFF: How come you never want to talk about her?

WIND: Because she's dead.

There's no point.

HUFF: But when you don't talk about her that kind of makes her . . .

What's the word teacher said?

Irrelevant.

And she's not irrelevant.

Not to me.

WIND: Will you stop being such a little bitch all the time?
Let those dry.
You wanna play the pass out game?

HUFF: Awesome!
Can I go first?

WIND: Yeah.

HUFF: Awesome!

WIND: *(to audience)* Ever played the pass out game?
It's where someone chokes you till you pass out.
What you do—if you want to try this at home—is grab your friend by
the throat, palms inward, and squeeze on his windpipe until the light
goes out in his eyes.

(to HUFF) Ready, little brother?

HUFF: Ready for blast-off!

> WIND *squeezes* HUFF's *windpipe shut until he falls asleep.* HUFF *is
> transported to his wildest dreams.*

TELEVISION HOST: Good'ay and welcome to *You Little Bitch*.
We're here today with the little boy with a magical power to give you the
feeling of laughter just by blowing.
When did you discover you had this incredible talent?

HUFF: My mom was all sad one day and I only meant to blow the hair
off her face.
She got real happy.

TELEVISION HOST: Amazing!
And you knew something incredible was happening.
Where's your mom now?

HUFF sees a woman in the audience!

HUFF: Right there!
In the front row.

TELEVISION HOST: Right here?
Hi, Tracey, how are you?

The TELEVISION HOST sits on her lap.

Oh no, that's not Tracey.
That's Donna.
She's just wearing your mom's sweater.
Don't you remember?
Your mom's dead.
In fact, it's probably about time you woke up.
Don't you think, "you little bitch?"

HUFF wakes up.

HUFF: Awesome!

WIND: Okay, little brother.
My turn.
Ready for blast-off.
Squeeze . . .
You gotta really squeeze tight.
Come on.
You gotta squeeze as tight as you can.

HUFF: My hands are too small.

WIND: *(to audience)* If your partner's hands are too small or if you're by
yourself you can still play the pass out game.
You just need a belt.
Like so . . .

WIND takes his belt off. He fits it around his neck.

Okay, little brother, pull.

    He does. Then:

HUFF: Abort!
Abort!
Charles is coming.

WIND: Oh fuck.
Charles.

    CHARLES enters.

CHARLES: They never found his head, you know?
Martin.
The hamster.
They never found his head.

    CHARLES removes the hamster's head from his pocket to show
    the boys.

I'll tell you know.
About the fire.
I'll tell Dad.

WIND: *(to CHARLES)* No, you won't.
C'mon, Charles.
That's not fair.
You were there too.

CHARLES: I'm not a retard.
I don't have FAS.

WIND: No, of course not.
That's just something we say.
For fun.

CHARLES: I'm not gonna tell.
Know why?

HUFF: Why?

CHARLES: I'm not gonna tell cuz you're gonna suck my dick.

WIND: Okay, fine, Charles.
We'll suck your dick.
Just please don't tell about the fire.

HUFF: I don't want to.

WIND: We have to.

CHARLES: Yeah.
Have to.
Get on your knees.

CHARLES inserts his penis into WIND's mouth.

Good.
Good.
Good.
Switch.

CHARLES inserts his penis into HUFF's mouth.

Good.
Do it better.
Good.
Good.
Take your pants off.

HUFF: Please don't make me.

WIND: Just do it.
It only hurt the first time.

CHARLES: Take your pants off!

CHARLES fucks HUFF. He takes his time.

WIND: *(to audience)* Charles pulls his pants up and leaves.
My little brother has a rug burn on his forehead.

(to HUFF) Hey, little brother, you wanna play Sega Genesis?

HUFF: Broke.

WIND: Oh yeah.
You wanna go shoplifting?

HUFF: No thank you.

WIND: Hey, little brother, I'm feeling kinda down.
I sure could use your sacred gift from Creator.

HUFF blows: whoosh. No effect.

HUFF: Any Lysol left?
Didn't think so.

MIKE: Boys—get in here!

Five, four, three—

WIND: *(to audience)* My dad is pretty mad.
You should probably go.

MIKE: —two, one.
LOOK AT THIS!

    MIKE grabs WIND by the hair.

THE BED IS RUINED!
THE COUCH IS RUINED!
YOUR DOG SPRAYED TOMATOES EVERYWHERE!

WIND: *(to audience)* Donna storms in with a white heel with red speckled on the toe and starts whoopin my ass with it.

    Smack! Smack! Smack! Smack! ANGELINA, loyal beast, springs into action! She sinks her teeth into DONNA's bare calf.

ANGELINA: Leave my brother alone!

MIKE: Angelina!
Let go.
Now!

ANGELINA: Fuck that!
I warned her!

    MIKE grabs ANGELINA by the collar.

MIKE: Angelina!
No!
Donna, you slammed my son down pretty fuckin good, don't you think?

DONNA: I didn't hit him.

MIKE: Yes you did.
I watched you.
We all did.

DONNA: That's not . . .
I just . . .
Why are you picking on . . .
I do . . .
I cook . . .
So your retard son can watch me in the shower!

MIKE: Charles!
Get down here.
Five, four, three—

CHARLES *enters.* MIKE *takes off his belt and beats* CHARLES.

CHARLES: Dad!
Stop!
Please!
Stop!
Please!
They started the fire!

MIKE: The . . . the fire?
At the motel?
You started that fire?

WIND: No . . . Charles, you snitch—

MIKE: You did.
And on top of that you lied to me.

HUFF: It wasn't his fault!
The flaming porno magazine turned into a raven—

MIKE: I don't wanna hear that word outta your goddamn mouth.

DONNA: Mike, don't.

MIKE *grabs her face.*

MIKE: Donna, shut the fuck up.
No one asked what you have to think.

DONNA: He's right, kids.
Confessing is the best thing for you.

WIND: *(to audience)* At just that moment the door opens and my kohkum arrives.

KOHKUM: Put that belt away!

MIKE: Kohkum, this is none of your business.
You shouldn't be here.

KOHKUM: My nosums are in trouble.
Smelling like Skunk on the moon of their mother's death.

MIKE: You're dementia!
This has nothing to do with the fucking moon.

KOHKUM: Don't you hit those kids.

MIKE: Kohkum, your daughter was a drunk.
She left you alone and me to take care of those boys.
I'm trying to do that the best way I know how.

KOHKUM; Nosums, listen to me.
You stay away from your dad when he's like this.
Shame on you, Mike.

MIKE: Old woman, you've had your head up your ass as long as I've known you.

KOHKUM: I'm not going anywhere, Mike.
You're going to have to throw me out.

MIKE: If that's the way you want it.

WIND: *(to audience)* That's when Donna takes me and my brother into the basement.

DONNA: It's okay, kids.
They're only fighting because they love you.
Now clean up!

WIND: Fuck.
Fuck.
Fuck.
Fuck.
Fuck.
Fuck.
Fuck.
Fuck.
Fuck.

HUFF: It's okay.
It's not so bad.
I got an idea.
Let's run away together.
We'll go to the woods and start a fire and everything and kill moose and live Indian way and then we'll go to Toronto and we'll show them our sacred gifts from Creator and we'll be famous.

WIND: That's the stupidest thing I've ever heard.
Wanna know why?

HUFF: Why?

WIND: Because no one cares about us.

> HUFF *points to the audience.*

HUFF: What about them?

WIND: Them?
They're not even real.

HUFF: Yes they are.

WIND: No they're not.

HUFF: Yes they are.

WIND: No they're not.
And neither is your sacred gift from Creator.

HUFF: Whoosh.

WIND feels warm inside.

WIND: Fuck off!

WIND pushes HUFF.

(to audience) That's when I run.
I throw my jacket on and run into the coldest storm of the winter.
My father and my kohkum fighting behind me.
The wind screaming through my clothes.

To the audience.

HUFF: *(to audience)* Hi?
Hi?
Hi.
I gotta keep cleaning.
Angelina's tracked tomatoes all down the steps and splattered them on the floor and the walls.
I got so much more to go.
It wouldn't be so bad if my brother were here to help me.
He didn't even bring anything for the cold.
Or to eat.

I should go find him.
Pack a bunch of stuff.
Nothing fancy.
Just what we really need.
My socks are wet.
Donna was wearing my mom's sweater yesterday.
Same dark hair.
Same red sweater.
I came in thought she was my mom.
I got real happy.
Gave her a big ol hug.
Then Donna turned around and my mom was dead again.
Ever real mean Trickster, hey?

Wind never sticks up for me.
I always stick up for him though.
If someone hits my brother they have to hit me too.
I don't care.
It only hurts for a second.
Only things people say hurt longer.
And stuff they do.

I better go find him.
He must be . . .
I don't know where he is.
We used to go to the motel.
But it's gone now.
Gone, gone, gone.
Sometimes I wish I were gone.

> HUFF *takes his belt off and makes a loop around his neck. He ties*
> *the long end to the doorknob.*

I can never remember the exact moment I fall asleep.
This time I will.
I'll think about my mom.
Down at the lake.

And how much I miss her.
And I hope you come back because then everything will be real good again.
Don't let me pass out for too long, okay?
Promise?
Blast-off!

    HUFF *hangs himself.* TRICKSTER *grabs the microphone.*

TRICKSTER: Thank you for listening to Shit Creek Radio, your voice for when you're up Shit Creek and you don't have a paddle.
The school is closed for the death of another one of our youth, the victim of apparent suicide.
A ceremony will be held for the family.
The whole community is welcome.
In the weather it's the first calm day for as long as I can remember.
Trickster.
Out.

WIND: *(to audience)* I spend the night in the stockroom of the store.
In the morning my kohkum finds me and tells me what my brother has done.

(to KHOKUM) No he's not.
No he's not.
He's not.
Because . . . we're going to burn the school down together.

(to audience) After that I see the world for what it is.
Angelina can't talk.
She's just a stupid dog.
Our mom never loved us.
She couldn't even love herself.
And no one gets a sacred gift from Creator.
After my brother dies I don't believe anymore.
And that's when my kohkum has the ceremony.

KOHKUM: Kaytayak miyna Awasisak Ka kiyow Kitatamskatinawaw!
Ahta O'sam Ayoskayouyake Oota Kitayanawaw.
Nikamok, Aykaya Kapayakapawit Napaysis.
Ah Nootch Katipiskak, Aykakiysimowa miyna Aynikamowa . . .
Aykiskisiya Ispiy Kakiy Wanihat O'siymisa.

WIND: My kohkum prayed all night.
After that she slowed down.
She didn't get sick right away but she didn't have that same bounce in her half-step anymore.
Like she left something in that ceremony for me.
And it worked.
For a while.

> WIND *goes to the audience member who saved him.*

I need that bag back.

I need that bag back.
I'm almost finished.
Can I please have my bag back?

> *If the audience member offers the bag,* WIND *refuses it. If the audience member keeps the bag:*

Thank you.

> *He returns to the stage. He turns back.*

> *He takes another plastic bag out of his pocket. He puts it on his head. He duct-tapes a seal around his throat.*

But no matter how many times you try and save me you can still find me here.
Not trying to take a plastic bag off my head.
Rebreathing the same breath until it chokes me.
Six minutes under.

See?

I told you.

There really is a perfectly rational explanation for all of this.

But this time I wish my little brother were here.

Because he could just come here and pick me up.

That's when it happens.

Tennis shoes.

Tiny and soggy-wet tennis shoes squeak across the linoleum floor.

Then a chair slides against the counter.

And as the tiny shoes disappear onto the chair out of sight—and as the cupboard door creaks open—and as the key to my handcuffs falls from the sky onto the floor in front of me I swear: I can smell tomatoes.

> WIND *unlocks the handcuffs and tears the mask off his face. He breathes. Whoosh.*

Breathe.

> *The lights fade out.*

STITCH

Stitch received its first workshop through Cahoots Theatre Projects in 2009 with dramaturgy by Jovanni Sy. It was performed by Michelle Latimer. Later in 2009, Alberta Aboriginal Arts read an excerpt at the first annual Rubaboo Arts Festival in Edmonton. The performer was Reneltta Arluk. VideoCabaret supported workshops in 2010 and 2011 with dramaturgy by Jovanni Sy. The performers were PJ Prudat and Cara Gee.

The play debuted at the Factory Theatre Studio, Toronto, as part of the 2011 SummerWorks Performance Festival, with the following cast and creative team:

Director: Jovanni Sy
Designer: Andy Moro
Performer: Cara Gee
Stage Manager: Nicholas Paddison

The play won the Spotlight Award for Performance as well as Theatre Passe Muraille's Emerging Artist Award for the script.

In 2011, Playwrights' Workshop Montréal facilitated a dramaturgical reading with Lois Brown. In 2015 Culture Storm remounted the work in the Aki Studio, Toronto, as part of Native Earth Performing Arts's 2014/15 season. The play was directed by Jovanni Sy, designed by Andy Moro, stage managed by Jen Stobart, and performed by Georgina Beaty.

Thanks to everyone who asked poignant questions, especially to Leanna Brodie and Tara Beagan, and to Yvette Nolan for speaking of hope.

CHARACTERS

Kylie Grandview

KYLIE covers her face with her hand.

KYLIE: You're sick.
I mean that.
You're disgusting.
I find you repulsive.
Do you see what I'm saying?
I would sooner let a cockroach inside me than you.
You're only here because you've had a derangement since birth that makes you get off on the worst on the Internet.
And let me tell you: the Internet is a big place.
But the ugly truth is that I need you.
I know: you're so pathetic; I can hardly believe it myself.
So I won't be asking much of you.
Just do what you always do.
Watch.
Because if you don't see this it's kind of like I never existed.
So put your hand on your mouse and click me.

KYLIE removes her hand to expose a terrible expression on her face,
a scar from the bottom of her top lip to the bridge of her nose. As
graceful as a dancer, KYLIE becomes the monster who cut her face.
The scorn becomes a smile as she returns to herself.

That's how this is going to go: like a porn video.
A stream of images flashing on a screen.
Part one of three: the story.
Part two of three: the build-up to some big climax.
Then just when you can't take it anymore there's going to be a huge explosion.

All over my face.
So click me.
You're all by yourself and I'm what you've always wanted.
I'm Kylie Grandview, the girl next door.
I'm Kylie Grandview, the cute lesbian.
I'm Kylie Grandview, your schoolgirl fantasy.
I'm interracial hardcore, double penetration, and a cum facial.
I come with heels, whips, and a yeast infection.
Click me.
I'm a mom you'd like to fuck.
Click me.
I'm the slave selling myself into freedom.

Click me at the boss's office.
This is my big moment: the box scene.
The one where I totally believe "Big-Time Agent" is going to make my
Hollywood dreams come true . . . if I suck his cock.
I'm about to roll in like I'm out of bubble gum when the director, Stephen
Steelcock, says:

STEPHEN STEELCOCK: Oh hey.
Kylie.
Leeya Springwood is here.
We're gonna double you guys with what's-his-name . . . Big Time.

KYLIE: This was going to be a boy/girl.

STEPHEN STEELCOCK: Yeah.
We didn't know Leeya was coming.
She just showed up.
Isn't that great?

KYLIE: Yeah, great.
Can I just go first?
Big Time can go twice, can't you, Big Time?

STEPHEN STEELCOCK: Big Time already went twice.
It'll be faster this way.

KYLIE: For you.
For me it's gonna take twice as long.
I have to pick up my kid.

STEPHEN STEELCOCK: Are we having a conversation right now?
Do I give a fuck?
Be in the movie or be picking up your kid.
Leeya's going to enter and threaten to sue for sexual misconduct in the workplace unless—

KYLIE: —she can suck his cock?

STEPHEN STEELCOCK: Yeah!

KYLIE: She's going to have trouble saying "liability."

STEPHEN STEELCOCK: That's not a significant factor for me.

KYLIE: *(to audience)* Click to one minute and seven seconds later.
The director says:

STEPHEN STEELCOCK: Go.

KYLIE: *(to audience)* And I say:

(having sex with her invisible partner) Oh god!
Oh god!
Fuck me!
Oh god, fuck me!
Oh god!

(to audience) I'm good at what I do.
Sex isn't part of the romance.
It's who I am.

Big Time fucks Leeya Springwood doggy style while she performs a humiliating and uninspired cunnilingus on me.

I writhe and moan and shiver with wave after wave of fake orgasms.

I'm just starting to go to that blank screen, not-really-there place when she says it.

One of those things that just knocks everyone right over.

LEEYA SPRINGWOOD: *(to Big Time)* Punch me.

Do you wanna punch me?

KYLIE: *(to audience)* The lighting guy looks over at the sound guy and we all look up at Big Time.

To see if he's going to do it.

I realize I'm looking at him for the first time.

Big Time looks up at the director as if to ask permission—and let me tell you: Stephen Steelcock is just falling over himself.

So Big Time punches her.

Gently.

A gentle rap with the side of his palm that makes her jump sideways and yelp a little.

This is just the kind of move that makes this a "Starring Leeya Springwood, Also Featuring Kylie Grandview" sort of thing.

After a few hits the director laughs and he stops.

But, oh no: she knows the rules.

If she doesn't, she's about to find out.

I ball up a fist and crack her in the side as hard as I can.

She yells in pain.

The director says:

STEPHEN STEELCOCK: Yeah, nice.

KYLIE: *(to audience)* So I crack her again in the same spot and then again, and again . . . then I get carried away.

I punch her again and grab her by the hair and jerk her over on her back.

I climb on the desk and pin her hands behind her back.

I slap her across the fucking face and then punch—

STEPHEN STEELCOCK: Stop.

LEEYA SPRINGWOOD: Owwwah!
Take it easy, you freak.

KYLIE: *(to audience)* I'm not embarrassed.
I love it.
I'm back on top and she knows it.
She's rubbing her side, feigning injury.
She's had worse in the trailer park.
Poor lamb.
Looking for sympathy in a room full of people who make pornography
for a living.
Sorry, there's only one way to get ahead in this business and that's not it.
Now it's my turn to take control of this movie.
I reach around to put—

(to Big Time) Are you having a problem?
He's having a problem.

STEPHEN STEELCOCK: Stop.
Don't worry about it, Big Time.
Take a break.
You've earned it.

KYLIE: I have to be out of here by two o'clock.
Where's the stunt cock?

STEPHEN STEELCOCK: Stunt cock's forty minutes out.
Why don't you help him?

KYLIE: Help?
He'll need more than help.
I've had abortions that were more fun to be with.

STEPHEN STEELCOCK: Tell him that.
I'm sure he'll find it very arousing.

KYLIE: *(to audience)* I get scolded for abusing the male talent, but come now, seriously.

They have one job to do and it's not as if it's that unpleasant.

Who wouldn't love to have their pizza delivered by me?

I had two enemas today.

I'm a team fuckin player.

Big Time's jerking himself raw and getting nowhere.

You'll have to believe when I say that performing mouth-to-cock resuscitation is not why I got into this business; but I can't be late.

When you're late to pick up your kid it's thought to be rude and inconsiderate.

When a porn star is late, it's "child abuse."

KYLIE whispers in Big Time's ear.

Shhh . . .

It's okay, baby.

(to audience) I take his penis into my mouth.

It's cold and wet and vaguely reminiscent of egg noodles.

I have to take one of Leeya Springwood's platinum blond hairs from my lips.

Then I stroke his chest while I suck his cock and I can feel Leeya laughing at me, but it doesn't matter what her or any asshole pornographer jack-off artist thinks of me.

Or anyone.

Either you love me or you don't exist.

Big Time gets hard and I climb on top of him.

KYLIE has sex with her invisible partner.

My eyes are open but I'm lost in space, uploading a little piece of my soul onto your hard drive.

I'm Kylie fucking Grandview, vroom fucking vroom.

I star in porn.

Excuse me?

Star.

And you know what?

It feels great.
The way it feels great to tell your boyfriend you cheated on him.

    KYLIE has sex with her invisible partner. She says to him:

Oh god!
I.
Love.
You.
I love you!

STEPHEN STEELCOCK: Stop!
Did you just say . . . what did you just say?

KYLIE: *(to audience)* The sound guy looks over at the lighting guy and
everyone looks up at me.

STEPHEN STEELCOCK: Right, whatever.
Haha.
Big Time, could you come on her face now, please?

KYLIE: *(to audience)* For this performance, I'd like to thank streak-free
foundation, makeup remover wipes, and my first grade teacher who
always believed in me.
Click me in Diane's bathroom.
I have to pick up my daughter.
We don't do bring-your-kid-to-work day in my family.

    KYLIE cuts a line.

Diane says she needs to "speak with me."
Which means she wants to remind me again that soon I'll be too old to
blow guys in videos and I'll have to do it at bus stops.
She means well.

    KYLIE bumps the line.

And it numbs the itch.

KYLIE scratches her vagina.

Oh, didn't I tell you?
I've got a persistent yeast infection!
You can work that into your fantasy if you want.
I call her "Itchia."
She starts with a small tingle.
Just to let me know she's thinking about me.
Then she heats up and burns.
Scratching only makes it hotter, but the need is insatiable.
And no matter what I try she just . . . won't . . . go . . . away . . .
She sears, and smokes, and whispers:

As graceful as a dancer, ITCHIA sears and smokes and whispers.

ITCHIA: Can I tell you something?
You're my best friend.
I know we've only known each other for five to seven days or whatever,
but I just know that we're going to be together for life.

*KYLIE bumps another line then cleans the residue off the toilet with
her finger. She deposits the remains in her top lip. The itch subsides.*

KYLIE: *(to audience)* I put my little vial on top of the vanity.
Click.

Her face goes numb. She tastes her lip.

I turn on the faucet to simulate handwashing.
This is nice.
I put my sunglasses on out of respect.
So Diane won't see me roll my eyes.
From the kitchen, shards of Diane still get through.
I'm carrying a little wrapped present that I bought for Ayla.

I always buy her tons of shit.
Click me in Diane's kitchen.

(to DIANE) You look good, Diane.

DIANE: Don't patronize me.

KYLIE: *(to audience)* My mother is very pretty except for black frown lines from always believing the worst about everybody.
Her smile is a twisted knot that says: you are going to hell when you die and I feel really good about that.

(to DIANE) Just trying to be nice.

DIANE: I'm in no mood.

KYLIE: I was thirty minutes late.
Traffic was ridiculous!

DIANE: Shut up!
Shut up!
Shut up!

>   *DIANE lowers her voice.*

This is very serious.
Your nine-year-old daughter has been teaching the neighbourhood children to have sex.

KYLIE: So what?
Kids tell each other about sex.

DIANE: I walked into the family room and found Ayla performing oral sex on the child who lives down the street.

KYLIE: Oral sex?
Are you serious?

DIANE: I am very effing serious.
That child is nine years old.

KYLIE: *(to audience)* . . . and I get this sick feeling in my stomach.
Click to Ayla in the family room—click back.

(to DIANE) What did you do?

DIANE: I bought them pizza and made them promise they'd never tell anyone.
Then I sent him home.

KYLIE: Really?
Just like that, huh?

DIANE: Yes, of course.
I told Ayla she has nothing to be ashamed of.
Nothing.
That it's not her fault.

KYLIE: Okay, good.

DIANE: It's her mother's fault.

KYLIE: Diane, fuck!

DIANE: That child is following you away from God!

KYLIE: Undermining me is going to fuck her up.

DIANE: Selling your sex is going to eff her up.

KYLIE: You were supposed to be watching her!

DIANE: Don't make this about me!
That child is crying for help!

KYLIE: This is about you!
This is all about Diane, Diane, Diane.
How many times was I sacrificed for your new boyfriend?
How many times was I standing alone while one of them—and you quit drinking and all of a sudden you're a decent human being?
I have news for you, Diane: that's not how it works!

DIANE: You're a prostitute, my daughter.
Are you listening to yourself?

> *KYLIE shakes her head, smiling. She's been holding this card for a long time.*

KYLIE: You know what, Diane?
I don't think Ayla needs to see you any more.

DIANE: Don't.
Don't you dare.
She needs me.

KYLIE: You're out.
Go practise acceptance or whatever you people do.

DIANE: You whore.

KYLIE: Is that any way to talk to your daughter?

> *AYLA enters. KYLIE's face changes completely as if DIANE isn't even in the room. KYLIE picks up AYLA and holds her.*

Ayla, snowflake, I missed you so much!

> *KYLIE mouths the words to DIANE over AYLA's tiny shoulder.*

You're out.

(to audience) Click me at home.
Our condo is on the thirty-second floor.
On rainy days the fog forms on the windows and it's like we live in heaven.
Ayla's feet sit on our glass coffee table.
She finished her Kids Meal.
Now she's drinking a vanilla milkshake.
She looks exactly like me, only smaller.

(to AYLA) Snowflake, I love you more than anything in this world.

> AYLA *slurps her milkshake.*

AYLA: Mom, what's a narcissist?
N-A-R-C-I-S-S-I-S-T.
Narcissist.
Diane says you're one, so I want to be one too.

KYLIE: A narcissist is someone who only loves themselves.
And I love you.
Diane doesn't know what that word means.

AYLA: Did I spell it right?

KYLIE: Yes you did.
You're a brilliant little girl.
Now, we need to talk.

AYLA: Am I in trouble?

KYLIE: No, of course not.
You didn't do anything wrong.
I'm not mad.

AYLA: Can I have my present?

KYLIE: Yes.

AYLA: Yes!

KYLIE: First, you need to tell me what happened with your friend.

AYLA: . . . We were playing "movie stars."
We found this movie.
We were trying some of the stuff.
We memorized the lines by heart so we could say them perfect.

KYLIE: Really?
Say some.

> *AYLA lifts her posture to recite, stops.*

AYLA: I don't want to.

KYLIE: Ayla, you tell me the truth, okay?
No matter what you're always going to be my snowflake.
Where did you get the movie?

AYLA: Under your bed.

KYLIE: So you've seen the movies under the bed.
You've seen me?

AYLA: Yeah.

KYLIE: Go get one.

(to audience) Click me on where I'm like: you don't know me!
You don't know me!
Because you don't.
Look, Oprah, I had no idea what to do.
I had to make it up, right there.

You've never even done a show about what to do when your nine-year-old audits your porn appearances.
I had to make it up right there.

Click back.
Ayla thumps back in.
She hands me a box: *Naughty Schoolgirls 11*.
I'm on the cover.
The movie clicks in and I strut into the classroom in a skirt and pigtails.
It's the one where I convince a teacher to raise my math grade . . . in exchange for sucking his cock.
Ayla knows every word.

AYLA: *(as teacher)* Kylie, you've fallen behind the rest of the class in math. I'm worried about your performance.

(as KYLIE) I'm doing my best, sir.
I really like math, honest.
It's just the way you teach is so boring.

(as teacher) I can teach it more interesting.

(as KYLIE) I think I know what you mean.

KYLIE: Ayla, this is what your mom does for a living.
It's my job.
It's how I feed you and pay for your toys.

AYLA: You're really pretty.

KYLIE: *(to audience)* On screen I take my shirt off and unzip his fly.

AYLA: I like when your hair was like that.

KYLIE: Ayla, none of this is real.

AYLA: Looks pretty real to me.

KYLIE: We're really having sex, but we're pretending to like each other.

AYLA: Doesn't look like he likes you.

KYLIE: These movies don't teach you about sex.
If you want to know about sex, ask me.

AYLA: Gross.
I already know about sex.

KYLIE: Then let me ask you a question.
Do you know what sex is for?

AYLA: Yes, duh.
It's about reproduction.
R-E-P-R-O-D-U-C-T-I-O-N.
Reproduction.

KYLIE: That is how you spell reproduction.
You're very smart.
Only that's not what sex is about.

AYLA: Yes it is.

KYLIE: Sex is about having a good time.
It's about fun.
When it's not done right it's not fun.
Do you think it's fun for me to raise you on my own?
It's not, snowflake.
I do it because I love you so much.

AYLA: Are you pretending now?

KYLIE: No, snowflake.
I'm not pretending.
Let me ask you something else.

Was it fun, with Cooper, or Tanner, or Cody, or whatever his name is?
Did you have fun?

AYLA: It felt like nothing.
Then Diane freaked out and yelled at us.

KYLIE: Was it fun when Diane freaked out?

AYLA: No, it was humiliating.
H-U-M-I-L-I-A-T-I-N-G.
Humiliating.

KYLIE: *(to audience)* On screen my math teacher pulls my hair and rubs my face into the carpet.

AYLA: *(as teacher)* Oh yeah!
You're a good girl.

(to KYLIE) That's why you do this?
It's fun?

KYLIE: Sometimes it's fun.
Sometimes it's not.
I do it for you, because I'd do anything for you: fun or not.

AYLA: I'd do anything for you too, Mom.

KYLIE: But you don't have to.
You can just be my snowflake, right?

AYLA: Right.

KYLIE: Good.
Now stop blowing the neighbour kid, okay?

AYLA: Okay.

KYLIE: Ayla, remember: I'm the only one you can trust.
Okay?
We're still best friends?

AYLA: Ya.

KYLIE: Forever?

AYLA: F-O-R-E-V-E-R.
Forever.
Can I open my present now?

KYLIE: Oh yeah.

>   *AYLA tears open the gift.*

AYLA: Awesome!
Kidoozie's My First Beauty Bag girls' playset features a hard, stylish travel case full with a detachable hand mirror, three curlers, a hair brush, a curling iron, and a motorized hair dryer that really blows air and hums! Everything you need to stylize your look.
Hair dryer requires two AA batteries (not included).
It's beauty time!

KYLIE: *(to audience)* She holds the mirror and blots foundation on her face in thick clownish gobs.

(to AYLA) Just a little.
You don't want it to be too heavy.
You still want to look like you.

(to audience) On screen the superintendent walks into the classroom for the double penetration.

AYLA: *(as superintendent)* How'd you like to get a little extra credit?

(as KYLIE) I think my wildest math-grade dreams are coming true.

KYLIE: *(to audience)* Here, in our living room in the sky, Ayla applies eyeliner and says:

AYLA: Now I can be pretty like you.

KYLIE: Click me at the clinic for sexual health.
This is all part of the fantasy, right?
Oooh, look at that hot girl with the yeast infection.
I'd like to see her get an AIDS test and a Pap smear.
I'm in the waiting room, trying not to scratch myself when this guy sits down across from me.
He's got specks of white in his dark hair; his baby blue eyes are looking right at me.

(to GUY) Hey.
What the fuck are you looking at?

GUY: I thought I knew you from somewhere.

KYLIE: *(to audience)* This happens.
People vaguely recognize my face everywhere I go.
One of the symptoms of being a porn star.
And the itch between my legs?
Well that's a symptom too.

GUY: You're Kylie Grandview, right?

KYLIE: You're a fan.

GUY: Yes.
Absolutely.
You're very beautiful.
Can I say that?

KYLIE: Of course you can.
That's why I do what I do.

GUY: Hey, listen, can I ask you something?

KYLIE: Well, I don't escort, you can't book me, and I'm not in the mood to sign any body parts.

GUY: No, no.
Not that.
This is going to sound weird.
Have you ever done any acting?
Like real acting.
Film or TV.

KYLIE: Do you mean to imply that the performances I give aren't real? Because I've trained years to attain the depth and versatility necessary to portray the complex range of characters I do.

GUY: Really?

KYLIE: Of course fake orgasms can't be taught.
You've either got the gift or you don't.

GUY: And you've got the gift?

KYLIE: You don't know the half of it.

GUY: The reason I'm asking is that I'm producing a film and the director is considering bringing an adult film actress on board.
You have an otherworldly face.
I'd love to hear you read.

KYLIE: You're right, it does sound weird.
Who are you?

GUY: I'm Guy.
Producer.

KYLIE: Guy Producer, you're trying to pick me up at the clinic for sexual health?

GUY: You shouldn't doubt yourself.
You could be extremely valuable to the project.
It's about this woman, Sophie, who's got all these people in her life who want to rescue her, only she doesn't need any help.
She's doing fine until their judgments get in the way.
We've got—

KYLIE: *(to audience)* —and he mentions this hot, young director.
A guy you'd know.

(to GUY) Well, it sounds interesting.

(to audience) He hands me his card.
"Producer."
He says he'll email me "sides."
Then he walks into his appointment.
I almost collapse I need to scratch myself so bad.
I guess this stuff happens every day.
I was already discovered once working in the drive-through window at McDonald's.
I could be rediscovered at the sexual health clinic waiting for anti-fungal cream.
Look how far we've come.

Click me at the Slippery Dick production office, the fluorescently lit lair of my not-pimp: Johnnie Cockring.
The office is crammed full of every type of porn you could possibly imagine.
The alkaline tinge of stale semen flavours the air.
Johnnie Cockring was once a smart kid out of law school.
He was married and on the fast track at some firm.
Only problem was his pro bono work.
His specialty was representing desperate sex workers in exchange for . . .
you get the picture.

He made a video about it back in the nineties and his wife divorced him and his firm fired him.
Now he represents porn stars.
Johnnie sits in his chair behind his desk in a black silk shirt that looks like it could be used to dress up the bad guy in a high school musical.
A few wispy strands of hair sit across his glistening bald head.
This cream really works.
Not a titch.

JOHNNIE COCKRING smells his fingers.

JOHNNIE COCKRING: Kylie, did you tell the stunt cock that you loved him today?

KYLIE: It wasn't the stunt cock but that definitely makes a better story.

JOHNNIE COCKRING: I laughed my dick-sack off when I heard that. Why'd you do that for?

KYLIE: Post-feminist expression.

JOHNNIE COCKRING: Kylie, you're special.
Like a beautiful . . . retarded kid.
I mean that in a nice way.
You get it.
Did you play nice with Stephen Steelcock?
That's an important relationship for me.

KYLIE: Yeah, fine.
While I've got your attention, can I talk to you about something?

JOHNNIE COCKRING cracks his knuckles.

JOHNNIE COCKRING: Oh good, yeah.
Business.
These guys from that website keep emailing.
They're doing the, ahem, forced entry piece.

KYLIE: I'm not interested.

JOHNNIE COCKRING: You sure?
It's a lot of money.

KYLIE: I told you, I don't care.
Those guys are creeps.

JOHNNIE COCKRING: Did you get a bad vibe off one of them?

KYLIE: *(to audience)* Johnnie Cockring likes me to believe that he has a really protective eye on me.

JOHNNIE COCKRING: Because if you got a bad vibe, just tell me.
We won't do it.

KYLIE: I don't want to get raped.
How's that?

JOHNNIE COCKRING: Oh, that.

KYLIE: Yeah, that.

JOHNNIE COCKRING: Kylie, can I be real with you for a second?

KYLIE: Please, Johnnie, be real.

JOHNNIE COCKRING: You've got a beautiful face.
But the pretty loses value.
These pervs . . . they've seen you do all the regular stuff.
There's less demand for it.
We've gotta start expanding your repertoire or . . . now if you can't do it you can't do it.
I'd never—look at me: I'd never ask you to do something you don't wanna do.

KYLIE: You ask me to do stuff I don't wanna do all the time.
Rape.
Urolagnia—

JOHNNIE COCKRING: This is not about urolagnia.
I mentioned urolagnia to you one time and you harp on it as if they're the only words I've ever uttered . . .
And it was a good opportunity . . . and I could still get it if you'd reconsider your fundamental position on—

KYLIE: Johnnie, fuck off.

JOHNNIE COCKRING: Just doing my job.
You wanted to talk to me about something?
What is it, a gig?

KYLIE: A movie.
But not a porn movie.
A movie movie.
I met this guy at an opening.
He said there was a part in something I could audition for.
He knows I do porn.

JOHNNIE COCKRING: I bet he does.

JOHNNIE considers, exploring his fingers with his nostrils.

This doesn't sound like something I'd be interested in.

KYLIE: Something you'd be interested in?

JOHNNIE COCKRING: Yeah.
This is one of those distractions.
You're talented.
Anyone can see that—and I mean anyone.
I just don't think this is a good idea.

KYLIE: You shouldn't doubt me.
I could be very valuable to them.

JOHNNIE COCKRING: Kylie.
How long have I known you for?
Where were you?
Working at McDonald's with that sexy fucking visor on.
Remember that?
What were you, nineteen?
Eighteen?
*Seven*teen?
You're like a daughter.
You're special to me.
I just don't want to see you get hurt.

KYLIE: You would let three guys piss on me but I can't do one audition?

JOHNNIE COCKRING: Yeah.

KYLIE: Why?

JOHNNIE COCKRING: Because it sounds like bullshit.
Kylie—you mean the world to me.
You're my best friend.
But you're no fucking movie star.
Okay?
Don't cry.
Please don't cry.

KYLIE: I'm not going to cry.
I'm going around you.

JOHNNIE COCKRING: We need to talk.
The company is called Slippery Dick.
It's not called Lippy Bitch.

You're out doing what you want to be doing and what you need to be doing is what I want you to be doing.
Or we're going to have to take another look at the face of this thing.

KYLIE: Can't you let this go?

JOHNNIE COCKRING: I could.
But why would I?

KYLIE: *(to audience)* He lets his words hang in the air.
As if I might not do it.
As if I might say:
"No, Johnnie.
This compromises my dignity.
This will make me feel bad for much longer than the two hours the shoot takes."

(to JOHNNIE) Okay, Johnnie.
I'll do the rape if I can do this other audition.

JOHNNIE COCKRING: All right!
That's my girl!

  KYLIE offers the card to JOHNNIE.

KYLIE: Here's his card.

JOHNNIE COCKRING: Oh, you're calling him yourself.

KYLIE: I am?

JOHNNIE COCKRING: Oh yeah.
I mean, unless you're willing to do something for me . . .

KYLIE: *(to audience)* He rolls his computer chair back, exposing that he's had his penis in his hands for our entire conversation.

(to JOHNNIE) No, thanks.
I'll call them myself.

> *With soft, moist fingers he recoils his penis, zips his fly.*

JOHNNIE COCKRING: Suit yourself; but, honestly, I have no idea what you see in those people.

KYLIE: Yeah I'm starting to think I'm a poor judge of character.

JOHNNIE COCKRING: Later.
Oh, Kylie?
I LOVE YOU!

> *JOHNNIE bursts out laughing.*

KYLIE: *(to audience)* Click me in the middle of the night.
Ayla's had a nightmare.

AYLA: I had a dream where you had to go away forever but it was so much money that you had to.
And I could never come visit, ever, no matter what, forever.
F-O-R-E-V-E-R.

KYLIE: Awe, snowflake, I would never do anything that meant I had to be away from you forever.

AYLA: Will you make pancakes?

KYLIE: It's three o'clock in the morning, snowflake.
You want pancakes right now?

AYLA: Yes.
Right now.

KYLIE: *(to audience)* I turn the lights on in the kitchen.
I take out a glass bowl and a frying pan.

AYLA: Mom, how come I don't have a dad?

KYLIE: You do have a dad: me, I'm your dad.

AYLA: You know what I mean though.
Who's my dad, reproduction-wise?

KYLIE: Your dad was a soldier.
We fell in love in high school.
And that's when you were born.
To take care of us, your . . . daddy went off to fight in the war.
And one day an IUD blew him up.
He was so brave and kind, how could I possibly ever love another?

(to audience) Click me on Oprah.
I know this probably wasn't the coolest thing to say, but the truth isn't
exactly going to make her feel like a beautiful, unique snowflake.
When she was born I told my fuck-wad high school boyfriend that she
was Johnnie Cockring's.
Then I told Johnnie Cockring she was my fuck-wad high school boyfriend's.
Neither followed up.
Click back.

AYLA: I miss him, you know.

KYLIE: He loved you very much.
And he's watching down from heaven.

AYLA: He saw me having oral S-E-X.

KYLIE: He forgives you.
Eat your pancakes, baby.

AYLA: I love you, Mom.

KYLIE: I love you too, snowflake.

(to audience) Click me in my big life-changing audition with Guy Producer, the handsome young studio exec.

In his private studio office, there's fruit and bottled water.

On the desk: a camera, always a camera.

Behind the camera: Guy Producer's warm blue eyes.

My crinkled photocopied sides have "Sophie" highlighted in blue.

"Sophie makes an Internet sex video to market herself."

I guess it never occurred to Sophie that making an Internet sex video only qualifies you to make more Internet sex videos.

I'm going to be perfect for this.

And then that thing, that little breath that starts somewhere deep, warms my diaphragm and dances up my spine and raises the hairs on the back of my neck: it's spreading into my knees, my feet, and my eyes are focused.

If I do this right everything changes forever.

F-O-R-E-V-E-R.

It doesn't get any more real than this.

I'm a breath away from being a movie star.

GUY: You look beautiful.

KYLIE: Tell me about your movie.

GUY: It's about this absolutely beautiful woman.

Ethereal, otherworldly..

She makes some fucked-up decisions and, sure, bad shit happens to her; but she refuses to be a victim.

KYLIE: *(to audience)* We read.

Fuck . . . acting . . .

Click me in the audition where . . . my big Hollywood dreams . . . are slipping away from me line . . . by . . . garbled . . . line . . .

Click to my yeast infection watching from the back row.

ITCHIA: OMG, you couldn't act your way out of a paper bag—which is exactly where you should be right now.

Where'd you learn to act?

Oh, right, the Royal Conservatory of Porn . . .
You better let me take this one.

KYLIE: *(to audience)* Click back.

(to GUY) I have an idea: Why don't we improvise a bit?

GUY: We really need to see the text as it's written.

KYLIE: I just feel like I can show you way more than what's written.

> She sits on GUY's lap.

Like, for example, don't you think this brings out a more intimate side
of me?
You don't have to squirm; I want you to be comfortable.
It's just you and me and the camera.
Aren't you going to love capturing this little moment forever and ever?

GUY: I guess so . . .

KYLIE: Cool.
And do you think it's just a little bit cooler if I move a little bit on top
of you?

GUY: That is cool.

KYLIE: Are you going to get me this part?

GUY: Uh . . . fuck it, why not?

KYLIE: *(to audience)* I do it.
I nail this role and I nail this producer, and I don't regret it for a second.
I walk into the sun, smiling.
Everything is going to be great.
I've got a hold on the mainstream.

I'm not just a porn star.
I am an actress.

Click me in my car.
I'm stopping at home to reapply the cream.
Itchia blows smoke in my face.

ITCHIA: Oh my god, if you think you can stop me with vaginal zit cream you have no idea who you're dealing with.

KYLIE: *(to audience)* Click me in my living room.
Something is wrong.
There are cops everywhere.
Diane is sitting on my sofa drinking tea.
Her key, her pick-up-Ayla-drop-her-off-any-time key, sits on the glass coffee table.
A woman in a pantsuit sees me.

SANCHEZ: My name is Detective Sanchez.
Are you Ayla's mom?

KYLIE: *(to audience)* Detective Sanchez has high cheekbones and broad lips that pop off the sides of her face, and she's talking really slow like I'm five years old.

(to SANCHEZ) Is she okay?

SANCHEZ: She's fine.
We came here and assessed that Ayla was in immediate danger.
Your mother found a vial of white powder in her bathroom today.
She was worried about you driving.
You look like you're in some discomfort.

KYLIE's been scratching herself.

KYLIE: Where is Ayla?

SANCHEZ: We did a test on that vial, which indicated heroin.
When we arrived here we found a similar vial in your bedroom.

KYLIE: Diane, you fucking bitch.

DIANE: You have no right to talk to me like that.

SANCHEZ: Please calm down.
You can't make this better right now; you can only make it worse.

KYLIE: You shameless fucking cunt!

(to audience) I lunge at her.
The cops tackle me.

DIANE: I have to do what's best for Ayla.
I always will.

KYLIE: You're psycho, Diane!
You're fucking crazy!

DIANE: You're a drug-addicted prostitute and unfit as a mother.

KYLIE: Click me while I get booked.
I'm locked in a windowless room under fluorescent lights.
I can imagine how my skin looks.
The Styrofoam coffee cup on the table has ink around the edges from
my fingerprints.

 ITCHIA smokes a cigarette.

ITCHIA: Now you've done it: you've lost your daughter.
You are worthless.
You are pathetic.
You are stupid.
Now you've done it: you've lost your daughter.
You are worthless.

You are pathetic.
You are stupid.
Now you've done it . . .

> KYLIE *scratches her vagina. The door opens.* SANCHEZ *clears her throat.*

SANCHEZ: Are you masturbating?

KYLIE: No.
I need my cream.
I'm scratching.

SANCHEZ: Where is it?

KYLIE: On my vagina.

SANCHEZ: I mean the cream.

KYLIE: In my purse.

SANCHEZ: They didn't give that back?
Hold on.

KYLIE: *(to audience)* I reapply in the bathroom.
Call it a touch-up.
Back in the windowless room, Detective Sanchez asks me if I'm good.
Then tells me:

SANCHEZ: State your name for the record.

KYLIE: *(to audience)* I tell her my information.
She stares at the screen.

SANCHEZ: Your daughter was remanded to state custody today when your mother found your drugs and assessed that you were driving impaired. Is that correct?

KYLIE: No, how about: my crazy psychotic bitch of a mother found her own drugs in her own apartment and was so wasted she forgot.
That woman is dangerous.
Put that.

SANCHEZ: Are you a sex worker?

KYLIE: Well then, here we are.
That's what this is about, is it?

SANCHEZ: This is about Ayla's well-being.

KYLIE: Then if it's for Ayla's well-being: yes.
I do porn.
I'm a sex worker, okay?
I pay taxes and my job is completely legal.

SANCHEZ: Do you think you provide an ideal atmosphere for a child?

KYLIE: Yes.
I do.
My daughter is loved.
She has a good home.
She eats well and does her fucking homework and Mommy has sex to pay for it all.
It's a criminal conspiracy and everyone's got their hands in.
Including you.
What's it take to snatch a woman's child from her?

SANCHEZ: Please.
My job is not to take your daughter from you.
It's to assess where the best care for her will be found.
It may, after a time, be with you.
But right now this hostility isn't helping.
You need to start telling me what I want to hear.
I don't enjoy every aspect of my job either.

KYLIE: I'd like to make a phone call.
But if you must know: I'm not just a porn star.
I act in real movies too.
I'm an artist, okay?
I do lots of projects.
If this were three months from now you'd be asking for my autograph.

SANCHEZ: Sign this, please.

KYLIE: No.

SANCHEZ: Then here's the phone.

The phone rings; JOHNNIE COCKRING *answers.*

JOHNNIE COCKRING: Slippery Dick Productions.

KYLIE: Johnnie, she's gone.
They took her.

JOHNNIE COCKRING: Who's gone?

KYLIE: Ayla.
I got arrested.

JOHNNIE COCKRING: Ayla's gone?
What'd you get arrested for?

KYLIE: Drugs.
It's nothing.
Diane called them.
They have nothing.
But, Johnnie, they took Ayla away.
They can't take Ayla away from me.

JOHNNIE COCKRING: Fucking cunt!
That fucking sick cunt!
Okay, you have to comply, and don't be hostile or aggressive in any way.

KYLIE: It's a little late.

JOHNNIE COCKRING: What'd you do, snowflake?

KYLIE: I called her a fucking sick cunt, or a psycho cunt, and I may have attacked her.

JOHNNIE COCKRING: What do you mean, "may have"?

KYLIE: I went Jerry Springer and attacked her with the cops everywhere. They threw me on the floor.

JOHNNIE COCKRING: Okay, don't do that again.

KYLIE: Can you help me?

JOHNNIE COCKRING: Yeah, anything for Ayla, you know that.
I'm gonna call this lawyer for you, Gloria Alright.
She's kept me outta more shit than sheepskin condoms.

JOHNNIE loves this joke.

She'll know what to do.

KYLIE: You can't handle this?

JOHNNIE COCKRING: Sure.
No problem . . .
If you'd like Ayla's case advocated by someone with a pending child-porn indictment.
In fact our relationship will probably already count against you . . . then your DUI, drug possession last year.

KYLIE: You took care of that.
It was "no big deal"?

JOHNNIE COCKRING: Well this is different.
Any time kids are involved.

KYLIE: Are we talking about Ayla or your child-porn thing?

JOHNNIE COCKRING: They found drugs in your house?
Was it a lot?

KYLIE: Can you pay bail?

JOHNNIE COCKRING: Absolutely.
But, snowflake, this isn't a good time for me.
You're gonna have to work it off.

KYLIE: Anything for Ayla, right?

JOHNNIE COCKRING: Call me with news, snowflake.

KYLIE calls AYLA.

AYLA: Hello?

KYLIE: Hi, snowflake.

AYLA whispers so DIANE won't hear.

AYLA: Mom!
I thought you were too sick to call me.

KYLIE: Sick?

AYLA: Diane says you're sick.
That's why we can't talk to you.

KYLIE: Snowflake, I'm not sick.

AYLA: Then why can't I come home?

KYLIE: Because Diane is a liar.

AYLA: So let's tell the truth.

KYLIE: We are but it's going to take some time.

AYLA: I hate her.

KYLIE: Me too.
We can't trust anything she says.

AYLA: I have to go—she's already going to know you called.

KYLIE: Snowflake—

DIANE intercepts the call.

DIANE: You are not to call here.
I am seeking a court order to restrain you from contacting us.
Goodbye.

KYLIE: Put her back on the phone, Diane!

Click.

(to audience) Click me in Gloria Alright's office.
She's a lawyer, a real one.
The kind whose cock you don't have to suck.
She has brown eyes and freckles, and presses her lips together while she
scribbles in black ink.

GLORIA: The quantity of drugs is troublesome because it indicates you
intended to distribute.

KYLIE: It was personal use.

GLORIA: That's not a significant factor for me.

KYLIE: What's going to happen to my daughter?

GLORIA: For now, Ayla's going to stay with Diane.

KYLIE: With Diane?
Why not with a pack of fucking hyenas?

GLORIA: It's the least disruptive situation.
The state will build its case against you.
They'll charge you with intent to distribute heroin, which carries a two-to-five-year sentence.

KYLIE: I could go to jail for five years?

GLORIA: That's not going to happen.

KYLIE: What do we do?

GLORIA: It seems peculiar that she'd call the police instead of requesting you seek addiction counselling.

KYLIE: That's because this whole thing isn't about drugs.
It's about porn.
She can't have me arrested for doing porn so she's having me arrested for doing drugs.

GLORIA: This is a personal vendetta.
Your mother—Diane has a problem with how you make a living—

KYLIE: And she's making me out to be some kind of fucking crack whore.

GLORIA: Okay, we should probably talk about court demeanour.
What to wear.

KYLIE: I'm a porn star, counsellor, not a retard.

GLORIA: Then you know you can't say things like porn star, retard, and fucking crack whore.

KYLIE: I can't say porn star?

GLORIA: We have to change the image people associate with you. You have to seem very present and reliable and not at all vacuous and entitled.

KYLIE: Are you saying I look vacuous and entitled?

GLORIA: Less in person. Is it possible that the drugs could have belonged to Diane?

KYLIE: Absolutely.

GLORIA: Would you be willing to raise that question in court?

KYLIE: Is Bill Cosby a rapist?

GLORIA: You said you're doing some regular acting? That's great. We're going to say that.

KYLIE: Okay, something else. Am I allowed to call Ayla?

GLORIA: Why wouldn't you be?

KYLIE: Diane said she was getting a restraining order.

GLORIA: I'll take care of that. Is it your name on the cellphone bill?

KYLIE: Yes.

GLORIA: Then you can call it all you want.
Listen, you have to show up at the hearing.
Leave the porn star behind.
Do that and we're going to get Ayla back home where she belongs and Diane is going to pay my fees.
Not you.

KYLIE: Whoa.

GLORIA: Now call that little girl and tell her she's coming home.

KYLIE: *(to audience)* Click me on the phone.

    The phone rings; ITCHIA answers.

ITCHIA: The number you are calling has been disconnected, please check the number and try your call again.

KYLIE: Ayla, can you hear me?
Everything's okay.
We can get you back.
You're coming back and everything is going to be beautiful, and full, and bright, and love.

    The hard, sharp disconnection dial tone throbs in her ear.

(to audience) Click to Ayla at home by herself.
She's streaming through a website, reading every word meticulously, writing in pink ink on a slip of paper.

Click to Itchia burning my hand with a cigarette.

    ITCHIA smokes a cigarette.

ITCHIA: You are so ugly.
Can you imagine if you looked on the outside the way you feel on the inside?

Would you even want to live?
I don't think so.
That's why we're meant to be together.
That's why where you go I go.
You know what I'm looking forward to?
The big rape scene.
Which reminds me, have you heard from Guy Producer?
Don't you think you should go over there?
He could fuck someone else on that couch and forget you even exist.

    KYLIE burns her own hand.

KYLIE: Please be nice to me.
It's so raw.
I just need a little break.

    KYLIE bumps a line. She is relieved for a moment.

(to audience) Click me at Guy Producer's private office.

(to GUY) Hey!
Guy!

GUY: Oh.
Hey.
I've been meaning to call you.

    KYLIE takes a nervous drags from a cigarette.

KYLIE: I left a message.

GUY: You left eight messages.

KYLIE: Sorry.
I'm just anxious to start talking with the director.

GUY: Kylie, listen.
We got some great news!
For the movie.
I guess not so great for you.
The movie got backing from a major studio last week and—they don't want the film to be represented by a porn star.
I fought for you in there.
It's just not the right face for them.

KYLIE: Not the right face for them?
Is this just something you do?
Lie to people and make them think that good things are happening to them when they're not?

GUY: I told you: it was just an idea.

KYLIE: So all I am is an idea to you?
Well I'm glad you got what you wanted.

GUY: Come on, don't be that way . . .
I gave you more credit than that . . .

KYLIE: Credit?
Credit?
You gave me more credit?

GUY: Maybe that's not what I meant to say.

KYLIE: I'm a porn star, so I should have enough credit to know you're a piece of shit liar.

GUY: Yeah.

KYLIE: Fuck you!

Click.

ITCHIA: OMG, you are so stupid.
I am personally ashamed to be your yeast infection.
And you know what I do when I get ashamed?
I get itchy, Kylie.
I get itchier and itchier and itchier and itchier.
I get so itchy you'll want to scratch my face off.

KYLIE: *(to audience)* Click me on the morning the cream stops working.

> *KYLIE grips the air, trying not to scratch herself.*

Of course it's never just any day the anti-fungal cream for the rash on
your vagina stops working.
It's also the day of the family services hearing, and the day I'm going to
be raped.
So I'm a busy girl.

> *KYLIE is bested by the agony of the horrible itch on her vagina;
> ITCHIA smokes a cigarette.*

> *KYLIE does a line.*

Click to Ayla packing her own lunch.
She's cutting the crusts off a peanut butter and jelly sandwich.
She's using a different knife to cut apples.
She's putting two juice boxes and three cookies into her pink lunch pail.

> *KYLIE falls asleep . . .*

> *KYLIE wakes in a terrified start.*

(to herself) Fuck!
Oh fuck!
What have I done . . .
What time is it?
Oh fuck!

KYLIE tears through a mess of laundry. She only has porn clothes ready.

Do I not have a single—
Where is that black . . . fuck!

She checks the time again.

Oh no . . .

She dons the porn clothes.

I'm supposed to be there now.
Like, right now.

(to audience) I grab the makeup kit with the little hand mirror and run out the door.
Click me in the car, on the way to court.
I forgot the dope at home.

(to herself) It's okay.
It'll be okay.
Mama doesn't itch now, snowflake.
It'll be okay.
Oh please, please, please be okay . . .

(to audience) Click to Ayla's third grade classroom.
Kids are yelling.
She wears her most responsible dress.
She's putting on rain boots and her raincoat.
She's wearing her knapsack.

A spasm of irritation!

Click me on Oprah, click me on Oprah, click me on Oprah.
This next part I don't want to say.

I'm giving you everything else; I'm giving you way worse; but this is the part that I want to bury, that I want to never see again.

Click me at the courthouse an hour late.
The glass doors hold my reflection.
I'm wearing a cardigan, three sizes too small, a miniskirt, and—oh my god: no underwear.
I see Gloria Alright.

GLORIA: Do you have any idea what time it is?
Jesus, we talked about what to wear, did we not?

KYLIE: What happened?

GLORIA: The court remanded custody to your mother.
What happened to you?

    KYLIE sees AYLA.

KYLIE: Ayla!
Ayla, snowflake, how did you get here?
I missed you so bad!

    AYLA jumps into KYLIE's arms.

AYLA: I took the bus all the way from school.
It was two hours.
I looked it up on the Internet.
I hate the Internet.
Can we go home, Mama?
I wanna go home.

KYLIE: Yes, we can go home now.
Let's go home.

(to audience) Diane walks towards us.

DIANE: Ayla, what are you doing here?
You're supposed to be at school . . . come on, let's go.
You have to come with me.

AYLA: But I wanna go with my mom.

KYLIE: *(to audience)* My lawyer is behind me saying:

GLORIA: Let's go.
We've got to walk away right now.

KYLIE: Okay, I've gotta go, baby.
Go with Diane.
Everything's going to be okay.

AYLA: No!

KYLIE: I'm always going to be your mom, okay, snowflake?
Always?

(to audience) Ayla looks at me for what I really am:

AYLA: You're a bad mother.

KYLIE: *(to audience)* I watch Diane take Ayla into a taxi and drive off.

(to GLORIA) So what now, is there, like, an appeal process?

GLORIA: I couldn't for the life of me think of what we'd appeal.
Look at yourself.
You need help.

KYLIE: Help?
Isn't that what I'm paying you for?

GLORIA: Check yourself into a treatment program.
You're very sick.

If you don't do that much, you won't see your daughter until she's eighteen.
But you should go anyway.
In the meantime, call me if you get arrested.
Good luck.

KYLIE: *(to audience)* Gloria Alright walks away; and Itchia whispers
smoke into my ear.

> *ITCHIA smokes a cigarette.*

ITCHIA: You so deserve this.
Now go get raped.

> *KYLIE drives to the rape.*

KYLIE: They told me to dress really young.
I'm still wearing my clothes from court—so this is perfect.

> *KYLIE gets out of her car and is choked from behind.*

(to invisible attackers) Cack!
I-cack!
Can't breathe!
I'm choking!

> *She fights the hands around her throat.*

Cack!

> *She struggles until she sees the camera. She collapses to the floor,
> her arms pinned behind her back. In a wretched twist of body parts
> she's forcibly unclothed; she gags and catches her breath before
> being choked again. KYLIE is raped. She poses and performs. When
> it's over, she sits up, defeated.*

(to audience) And then it's over.
And they thank me.

And they pay me cash.
One of them actually laughs while he says it's great to work with me.
They tell me I'm a real pro.
They tell me I've got presence.

Click me at home for the big climax.
Part three of three: Itchia and me, both vying to see who gets to be the star of this movie.
Itchia cuts lines on the couch but won't share them with me.

ITCHIA: You're gross when you're high.
I can't believe you did that.
I wouldn't have done that.

KYLIE: You told me to!

ITCHIA: OMG, you're right!
I did.
I am such a bitch.

KYLIE: Who do you think you are?

ITCHIA: A better question is: Who do *you* think I am?

KYLIE: Shut up.
I'll kill you.

ITCHIA: No you won't.
You made me!
If I'm gone who will clean up your little accidents?
Who will pick up the pieces?
Who will stitch you back together?

KYLIE: Itchia, I will cut you out of me.

ITCHIA: Wake up!
This is not about your vagina.

This is about you and me and love, love, love.
Do you see what I'm saying?
Why don't you look?

KYLIE: *(to audience)* She hands me Ayla's mirror: I see Kylie Grandview.
I realize I'm looking at her for the first time.

> KYLIE *stares into her reflection. She's the monster who cuts her face.*
> *She smashes her face with the mirror. Her hand covers the wound.*

I don't want to move my hand.
I don't want to see.
Oh my god.
My face.
My face.

Click me in front of the bathroom mirror.
It's one of those days: when your hair won't do what you want it to and
your face is gushing blood.

> KYLIE *slowly removes her hand to see the terrible wound: a deep*
> *cut from the bottom of her top lip to the bridge of her nose.*

Torn.
Oh my god.
The flesh is torn.
My face is torn.
The glass cut right through . . . torn.

> KYLIE *becomes fascinated with the wound on her face.*

(to audience) Big, thick drops of blood fall off my fingers and splatter
onto the floor.
Click.
Click.
Click.

(to herself) I have to go to the hospital.

> *She giggles.*

I'm bleeding like a motherfucker.

(to audience) In the closet there's a baseball hat and a pair of sunglasses.
I can drive myself to the clinic.
No one will see my face.
Tomorrow, I'll be Kylie Grandview again and no one will see my face . . .
but then I see myself in the broken shards on the floor, thick blood dripping from my lips: fuck me, you are gorgeous.

Instead of my disguise, I pick up my sewing kit.
There are ten compartments but for some reason I only have black thread.

> KYLIE *sits on the floor. Her hands shake while she threads the needle.*

(to herself) Fuck.
Fuck.

> *She ties the thread on her second attempt. Her knees shake.*

You can do this.

(to audience) I bump a line off the sink.
Blood from my face drips onto the powder and crystallizes.
Little red snowflakes.

> *She does another line and picks up the needle and thread. She faces herself in the bathroom mirror. She plunges the needle into her flesh, just under the nose. She takes a quick breath and then plunges the needle into her face again for the next hole. Her whole body shakes as if she were hypothermic. She plunges the needle back into her face for the last stitch.*

Then, as if to a lover for the first time:

Hi.

The lights fade out.

*KYLIE picks up the phone and dials 9-1-1. The operator picks up.
It's ITCHIA:*

ITCHIA: 9-1-1 Emergency.
Please state the nature of your big me, me, me tragedy.
Hello?
Who is this?

The lights fade back in. KYLIE is covering her face with her hand.

KYLIE: *(to audience)* Epilogue!
Time to dish out all the gross details.
The doctors said that the shards of mirror broke on the bridge of my nose
and sliced through my face causing lacerations to the levator labii right
down through the orbicularis oris.
My stitches infected in gangrenous green and black streaks overnight.
But that was perfect, because I want my face to be one you can't forget,
even though you want to.

She removes her hand, starts again.

Do you recognize me?
Or are you looking at me for the first time?
Does it ever feel like you're waiting for something big to happen and it
just never does?
Well this is another one of those days.
But not for me.
For me, today is going to be different.
Today I'm taking another look at the face of this thing.
Today is my very last performance.
So if this gets you going.

Go ahead.
Click me.

The lights fade out.

End of play.

Cliff Cardinal is a multiple-award-winning Indigenous playwright and actor. Before graduating from the playwriting program at the National Theatre School of Canada, Cliff wrote three solo plays, including *Huff* and *Stitch*, both of which garnered him awards. In addition to his work in theatre, he also has a music project called Cliff Cardinal and The Skylarks, who recently released their debut album *This Is Not A Mistake*. Cliff lives in Toronto.

First edition: March 2017
Printed and bound in Canada by Imprimerie Gauvin, Gatineau

Cover photo of Cliff Cardinal by akipari provided courtesy of Native
Earth Performing Arts

**PLAYWRIGHTS
CANADA PRESS**

202-269 Richmond St. W.
Toronto, ON
M5V 1X1

416.703.0013
info@playwrightscanada.com
www.playwrightscanada.com
@playcanpress